COLOURING OUR ZODIAC™

A Therapeutic Experience

by

Shu-Ann Hoo

PREFACE

Almost 2 decades ago, my grandfather suffered from dementia and had to spend his remaining years confined at home. As his memory faded, he had difficulty recognizing his family members. It was sad to see him withdrawn and losing the will to live.

I began reading up on dementia, Alzheimer's and other chronic neurodegenerative diseases and discovered they often started gradually and worsened over time. The most common early symptom was difficulty in remembering recent events. As the disease advanced, other symptoms could include problems with speech, mood swings, disorientation, loss of motivation, and a whole list of behavioural issues. As neurodegenerative disease is hereditary, I became even more concerned about my family members' mental health especially as they reach retirement age. I realized keeping them occupied with daily activities, wasn't enough stimulation for their brains. So I created Colouring our Zodiac™ as a form of cognitive therapy for them and was pleasantly surprised at how they had benefitted from it.

Besides creating beautiful images with intricate patterns for you to colour and focus on, each image is accompanied by a page opposite for you to express your thoughts in writing because expressive writing has been linked to improve your mood, well-being, and reduces stress levels.

At a personal level, whenever I was faced with stress that often triggered my anxiety attacks, I turned to Colouring our Zodiac™. It helped me escape into a world of creative expressions as I relate the Zodiac animals with everyone I cared about and that made me feel calm and relaxed. This book has also increased my oldest son's self-esteem and his sense of personal well-being. It inspired his creativity and appreciation for art and his surroundings. As for my other boys, Colouring our Zodiac™ helped calm their emotions, managed their anger and increased their attention span, which led to better grades in school. Best of all, it made them more independent and confident in their problem solving skills.

What started out as an experiment for my family ended up providing us with a great deal of positive experiences. Most important of all, Colouring our Zodiac™ brought my family, both young and old, closer together.

Canada is now my home and I'm very grateful for all the opportunities I've received. I'm pledging part of the proceeds from Colouring Our Zodiac™ to the Canadian Mental Health Association as my way of giving back to this amazing country.

I hope this book brings you as much joy and positive experiences as it has to my family. Let's build and strengthen relationships, love and inspire one another through colouring therapy.

Shu-Ann Hoo
OohSA Productions

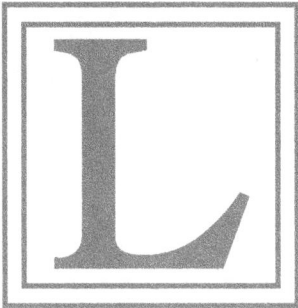

L egend

has it that one night before the Chinese New Year, the Jade Emperor summoned all the animals to participate in a race to commemorate his birthday. He wanted to appoint them in a way to measure time in a 12 year cycle. However, with so many turning up, he decided that the first 12 would have a year named in their honour according to the order they finished the race. It was a long and undulant one passing through dense forest and rough waters.

The Cat and the Rat were worried for they were not strong swimmers. They hitched a plan to ride on the back of the Ox, promising to let him finish ahead of them. The Ox being a naive and good natured animal, agreed and carried them across the river. But the cunning Rat pushed the Cat into the water, and jumped off the Ox to finish first. The kind Ox came in second.

Shortly after, an exhausted Tiger made his way to the finished line. The King of all creatures had struggled against the strong currents. But with sheer determination, he made it. The Emperor was so pleased with his efforts that he named the Tiger the third animal under the Zodiac.

Meanwhile, from a distance came a thumping sound. The Rabbit hopped her way to make it forth. She claimed she had made good use of rocks and stones to take her across the river. But it was later revealed she was helped.

The powerful and mystical Dragon who could easily fly across the river, explained to the Jade Emperor he was delayed because he helped put out a village fire and relieved another of a drought. He also helped a Rabbit who had fallen into the river, clinging for dear life on a log. The Dragon blew against the current to push the Rabbit to shore.

The Dragon's generous and kind acts, pleased the Jade Emperor and was designated the 5th Zodiac animal. Up till today, the Dragon year has been favoured by everyone and many couples wish to have a child born during the year of the Dragon.

The Emperor then heard the sound of a Horse's neigh as he galloped and neared the finishing line, the Snake jumped off from the Horse's hind legs and slithered ahead. The poor Horse had to be satisfied with 7th place. Soon after, a raft carrying the Goat, the Monkey and the Rooster reached shore. They told the Jade Emperor it was teamwork that got them to the finishing line. The Rooster shared the raft he found with the Goat and the Monkey clearing the weed as they steered their raft to shore. The Jade Emperor was impressed with their team effort and appointed the Goat as the 8th animal, the Monkey the 9th, and the Rooster, the 10th.

The next to finish was the Dog. The Jade Emperor was puzzled why the Dog took so long as he was a good swimmer. The Dog replied that the water was so refreshing, he got carried away splashing and playing in it. He was rewarded the 11th place on the Zodiac.

Now with only 1 place left to complete the 12 animal cycle in the Chinese Zodiac, the Jade Emperor wondered when the last winner would arrive. He had nearly given up when he heard a grunt and asked the Boar what had caused the delay. The Boar sheepishly said he was hungry along the way and decided to grab a bite. But he over ate, fell sleepy and took a nap. The Jade Emperor was still pleased the Boar finished and named him the last animal in the Chinese Zodiac.

As for the Cat who was pushed into the water by the Rat, he finally made it to shore. Unfortunately, he was too late to make it as one of the 12 winners in the race. The angry Cat was so mad at the Rat that since then, they never got along.

Year of the Rat 鼠(Shǔ)
1924, 1936, 1948, 1960, 1972, 1984, 1996, 2008, 2020
You are wise, adaptable, and outgoing
You are compatible with those born in the year of
the Rabbit, Dragon, Monkey, Dog, and Boar

Year of the Ox 牛(Niú)

1925, 1937, 1949, 1961, 1973, 1997, 2009, 2021

You are industrious, honest, and patient

You are compatible with those born in the year of

the Rat, Rabbit, Snake, and Rooster

Year of the Tiger 虎 (Hǔ)

1926, 1938, 1950, 1962, 1974, 1986, 1998, 2010, 2022

You are intelligent, loyal, and virtuous

You are compatible with those born in the year of

the Horse, Dragon, Rooster, and Dog

Year of Rabbit 兔 (Tù)

1927, 1939, 1951, 1963, 1975, 1987, 1999, 2011, 2023

You are amiable, compassionate, and sensitive

You are compatible with those born in the year of

the Rat, Ox, Sheep, Dog, and Boar

Year of The Dragon 龙 (Lóng)

1928, 1940, 1952, 1964, 1976, 1988, 2000, 2012, 2024

You are ambitious, decisive, and inspiring

You are compatible with those born in the year of

the Rat, Tiger, Dragon, Monkey, Rooster and Boar

Year of The Snake 蛇 (Shé)

1929, 1941, 1953, 1965, 1977, 1989, 2001, 2013, 2025

You are determined, passionate, and sympathetic

You are compatible with those born in the year of
the Ox, Snake, and Rooster

Year of the Horse 马 (Mǎ)

1930, 1942, 1954, 1966, 1978, 1990, 2002, 2014, 2026

You are warm-hearted, energetic, and adaptable

You are compatible with those born in the year of
the Tiger, Sheep, Dog, and Boar

Year of the Sheep 羊 (Yáng)

1931, 1943, 1955, 1967, 1979, 1991, 2003, 2015, 2027

You are considerate, hardworking, and persistent

You are compatible with those born in the year of

the Rabbit, Horse, Sheep, Monkey, and Boar

Year of the Monkey 猴 (Hóu)
1932, 1944, 1956, 1968, 1980, 1992, 2004, 2016, 2028
You are confident, innovative, and sociable
Your are compatible with those born in the year of
the Rat, Dragon, Sheep, and Dog

Year of The Rooster 鸡 (jī)

1933, 1945, 1957, 1969, 1981, 1993, 2005, 2017, 2029

You are capable, independent, and warm-hearted

You are compatible with those born in the year of

the Ox, Tiger, Rabbit, Dragon, Snake,

and Horse

Year of The Dog 狗 (Gǒu)

1934, 1946, 1958, 1970, 1982, 1994, 2006, 2018, 2030

You are courageous, faithful, and lively

You are compatible with those born in the year of

the Rat, Tiger, Rabbit, Horse, Monkey, and Boar

Year of The Boar 猪 (zhū)

1935, 1947, 1959, 1971, 1983, 1995, 2007, 2019, 2031

You are gentle, honest, and loyal

You are compatible with those born in the year of

the Rat, Rabbit, Dragon, Horse, Sheep, and Dog

www.ingramcontent.com/pod-product-compliance
Lightning Source LLC
Chambersburg PA
CBHW081234020426

42331CB00012B/3170